Trenes

Ursula Pang

Traducido por Esther Sarfatti

PowerKiDS press

PK Principiantes

¡Ya viene el tren!

2

Ten cuidado con los trenes.
¡Los trenes son grandes y rápidos!

5

Los trenes pueden tener muchos vagones.

VAGÓN

Los vagones de tren tienen muchas ruedas. Las ruedas se mueven por las vías férreas.

RUEDA

VÍA FÉRREA

El primer vagón
es la locomotora.
La locomotora jala
los demás vagones.

11

El conductor de un tren se llama maquinista.

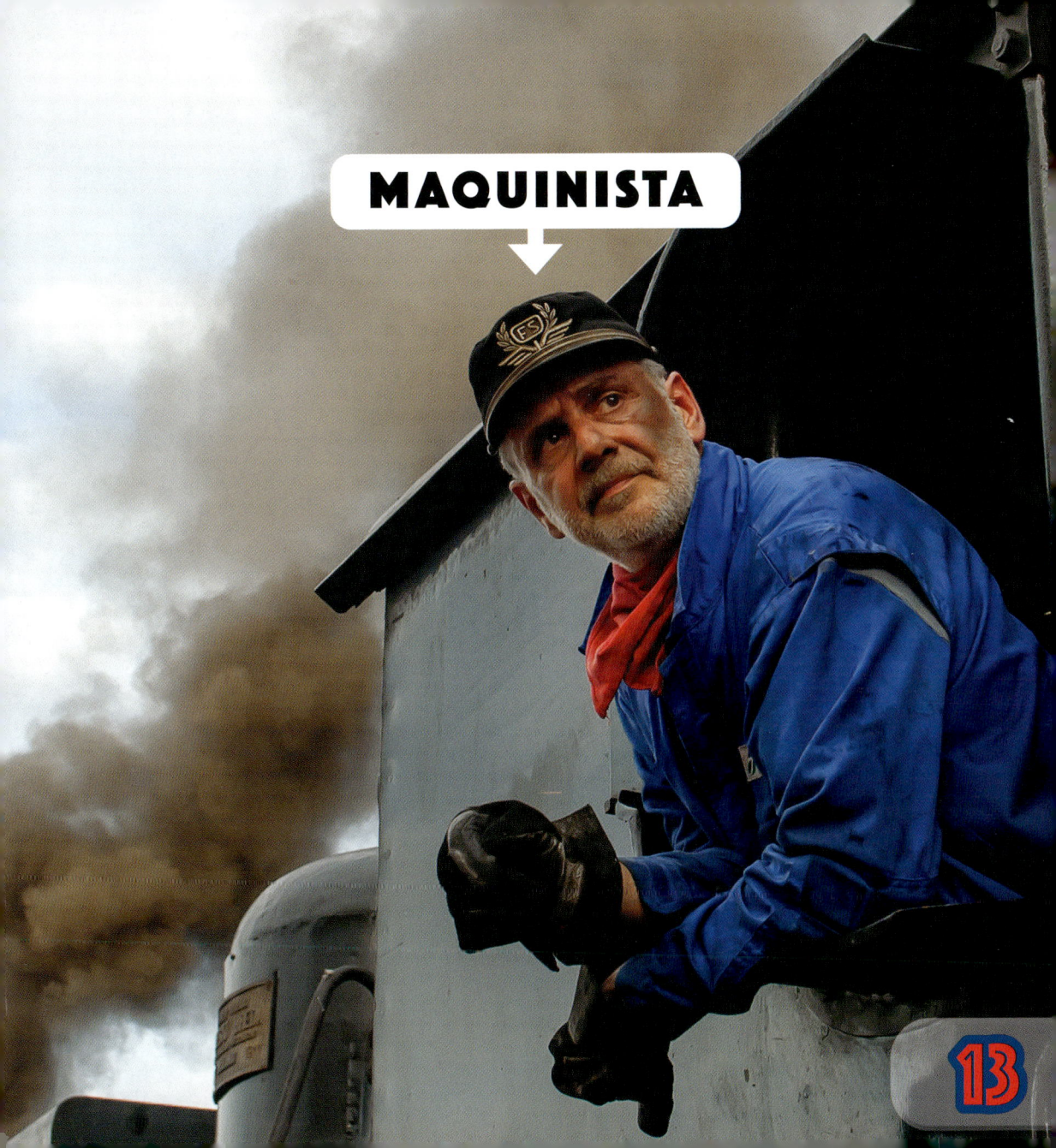

MAQUINISTA

13

Algunos vagones tienen asientos para la gente. Quedarte en tu asiento es lo más seguro.

15

¡El metro es un tren subterráneo!

17

Algunos trenes llevan mercancías. Las mercancías se llaman carga.

CARGA

19

Algunos países tienen trenes bala.
¡Son muy rápidos!

21

¿Alguna vez has viajado en tren?

23

Harris County Public Library, Houston, TX

Published in 2025 by The Rosen Publishing Group, Inc.
2544 Clinton Street, Buffalo, NY 14224

Copyright © 2025 by The Rosen Publishing Group, Inc.

All rights reserved. No part of this book may be reproduced in any form without permission in writing from the publisher, except by a reviewer.

First Edition

Editor: Greg Roza
Book Design: Rachel Rising

Photo Credits: Cover, p. 1 Boxcar Media/Shutterstock.com; p. 3 kwanchai.c/Shutterstock.com; p. 5 travelview/Shutterstock.com; p. 7 Guitar photographer/Shutterstock.com; p. 9 Raman Venin/Shutterstock.com; p. 11 lihaoming1234567/Shutterstock.com; p. 13 esherez/Shutterstock.com; p. 15 talyonen/Shutterstock.com; p. 17 Marek Masik/Shutterstock.com; p. 19 nattanan726/Shutterstock.com; p. 21 Sean Pavone/Shutterstock.com; p. 23 Gladskikh Tatiana/Shutterstock.com.

Library of Congress Cataloging-in-Publication Data

Names: Pang, Ursula, author.
Title: Trenes / Ursula Pang.
Description: Buffalo : PowerKids Press, (2025) | Series: En marcha
Identifiers: LCCN 2023051600 (print) | LCCN 2023051601 (ebook) | ISBN 9781499447989 (library binding) | ISBN 9781499447972 (paperback) | ISBN 9781499447996 (ebook)
Subjects: LCSH: Railroad trains--Juvenile literature. | Railroad trains--Parts--Juvenile literature. | CYAC: Railroad trains. | LCGFT: Instructional and educational works.
Classification: LCC TF148 .P35 2025 (print) | LCC TF148 (ebook) | DDC 625.2--dc23/eng/20231120
LC record available at https://lccn.loc.gov/2023051600
LC ebook record available at https://lccn.loc.gov/2023051601

Manufactured in the United States of America

Some of the images in this book illustrate individuals who are models. The depictions do not imply actual situations or events.

CPSIA Compliance Information: Batch #CSPK25. For further information contact Rosen Publishing at 1-800-237-9932.

Find us on